Opia

Alan Moore

Opia

Anvil Press Poetry

Published in 1986
by Anvil Press Poetry Ltd
69 King George Street London SE10 8PX
51 Washington Street Dover NH 03820

Set in Ehrhardt
by Bryan Williamson, Swinton, Berwickshire
Printed in Great Britain
at the Arc & Throstle Press
Todmorden, Lancs

This book is published
with financial assistance from
The Arts Council of Great Britain

British Library Cataloguing in Publication Data

Moore, Alan
  Opia.
  I. Title
  821'.914   PR6063.059/

  ISBN 0-85646-161-X

Library of Congress Cataloging-in-Publication Data

Moore, Alan, 1960-
  Opia.

  I. Title.
  PR6063.059406   1986   821'.914   85-30814
  ISBN 0-85646-161-X

TO
MY GRANDFATHER
GERARD MOORE

VALENTINE That man that hath a tongue, I say is no man,
if with his tongue he cannot win a woman.

DUKE But she I mean is promised by her friends
unto a youthful gentleman of worth
and kept severely from resort of men,
that no man hath access by day to her.

VALENTINE Why then, I would resort to her by night.

The Two Gentlemen of Verona III.i

ACKNOWLEDGEMENTS

Acknowledgements are due to the following, where some of these poems first appeared: *In Touch* (Hodder and Stoughton), *New Irish Writing* (The Irish Press), the *Poetry Ireland Review*, *Public Sector Times*, the *Sunday Independent* (Poem of the Month), the *Taxes Record* (Irish Tax Officials' Union), the *Times Literary Supplement*.

CONTENTS

GIRLS' SCHOOL

March beyond green outskirts:
clouds are blousy dawn-flirts....

A long school scarf, the driveway
trails the feet of chestnut trees.
Behind oaks, radios seem to be being tuned.
Birds study their toes.
Down in the hockey field, the gardener
sits like a monkey on a mower
that exhales green exclamation marks,
his jacket limp on the lawn, a dead dog.

Chatter echoes in corridors. Coats conspire.
Every locker hoards its pair of milk-white sneakers.
Under cover of a desk, twin apples let go their scents.
Pencils throstle in a nest.
A hedgehog hairbrush peeps from a handbag.

In the gym, Hitler mädchen
sit crosslegged around flasks and sandwiches,
little Marilyns, winking their approval
of *Meatloaf* and *Adam and the Ants*,
the wispy titles that tattoo
their camouflaged satchels.

Outside, under crimped zinc,
dewy bicycles mount. Spokes glitter.
Whichever elm is examined, silver lacework trembles,
leaves sway in an Austrian wedding waltz,
leaf-light cascades like confetti.

With a torturer's tongs, his brogues clinching gravel,
the gardener snips carefully at a fringe
where snowdrops present themselves like debutantes.
He picks one gently, smiles like a Pope.

WELCOME TO DUBLIN

I

At the airport, a hug.
August stars, we walk.
A foggy room:
people drinking, laughing.

Later, I creak
the door to a close.
Those roguish eyes:
"You want we make *Love*?"

Daylight. I stare
at that red skirt
folded on a chair,
inhale Gauloise,

chestnut hair.
I carry your cases.
At the airport, you shrug.
"Don't be *Romantic....*"

II

A jet hawked in blue
high over Dublin Castle.
In Tallaght, poppies were seen.
We were eating salad.

Pink clouds, rusted light on old
school bricks, birds blown away
like fluttered cigarette ash.
Ants massaged a crumbling wall.

In all their presses, naked cups
and plates hid from lightning.
Levi-Strauss jeans reclined upon a bed.
An insect zip looked up inquiringly.

THE PIRANHAS

"We have two. That's Brian over there,
and this is Fred," the white-coated
young man said. Fist-sized, moping
about his container, gloomily alone,
a villainous toad-brown "mouth
with a body attached." "Fred hasn't
been fed for about a month."
Dolefully, Fred looked at the orange
forms in the tank next door.
"What does he eat?" "Goldfish mainly,
but we're trying to get him off them.
Poor old Fred. We'll give you a little
one." Indulgently, he dropped a small
goldfish in. The goldfish became
freakily active, and tried to jump
out. "Fred'll let him tire himself out
first." Then, in one go, the goldfish
was gulped up. A tail-fin wiggled
momentarily between the tiny teeth
that formed Fred's lips. "Well, sir,
are you interested in giving Fred a home?"

THE MEANING OF THE WORD 'LUST'

I

Blonde log-fire smoke.
A soiled flag crumples
beneath a cannon.
The fields heave
their bloodied wheat.
Soldiers lurch and cough.

One man stands alone
with hands behind his back.
He brushes aside veils
of freezing fog, as though
to enter a woman's bedroom.
The wind whips his coat-tails.

II

Seamy with my foxy lady.
Some fumbling is inevitable.
Then, the usual drumroll,
a clash of cymbals, wonder
at suddenly exploding fireworks,
all the after-scatter of sparks.

How high the sprinklings are.
This girl's happiness is inside tonight.
It is no fiend who tears the air.
Muscular clouds wrestle
with the vigour of fierce horses
let loose. Flung crockery.

TREES

Some hail you from a great distance,
like friends not seen for years:
others are recluses, complete weirdos,
living alone on mountain-sides.

Some conspire in close groups,
and tell old widows' tales:
others gossip to whoever will listen,
and insistently nod their heads.

Some are solitary sentries,
shuddering in their green great-coats:
others, less soldierly, tremble
at the least push, and start to cry.

Some are dictators, making frenzied
speeches to audiences of daisies:
others, neither tyrants nor idiots,
make humane gesticulations.

Some throw coins of burnished copper
into lakes whose magic has died:
others are ballet dancers,
content with the simplest gestures.

Women, their imagined lover is wind,
who kisses them lingeringly:
men, often angry with themselves,
they throw everything up in despair.

THE MATCHBOX

If agitated,
it is a castanet.
Let it sit.

It is a little drawer
packed with pink-haired splinters,
excitable pine poker raspers,

heretic mop-heads
dripped in luminous
paint that tingles.

It is a strip of sand
in Mexico, gold gravel and
magenta burn-marks,

all the white faces
who last saw a small hiss,
blue flare, shoulder wall.

This prison yard
chorus mourns
a charcoal twiglet

that claws
feebly as a foetus,
coughing gravely....

FLÜNTERN

Summer evening, warm, dull.
Exhausted brambles loll
by a worn wall.

Each crumbling cross,
every tall tombstone, is
camouflaged in moss.

Day's grassy smell
is fresh still:
dusk begins to chill.

Ticks over the red hill
are really swallows: all
muscle, muscle, till

fall of fog. I turn
freely and discern
petals that burn.

Last light on trays of sugar.
I find a poppy, flung here
by some distraught visitor.

Sycamores shrug. Cool silence.
I hope without sense
to breathe dead fragrance.

The odour died when it was born.
This rusty graveyard gate
says what I cannot: *forlorn*.
A weird moan. I am too late.

THOUGHTS IN A LECTURE

We are sitting like the heads
on Easter Island, monks
etching at their scripture,
oblivious of each other.

In Merrion Square,
you dabble at your typewriter,
paint milk on ants you crush.
I see your amber hair.

A small army-green
transistor radio
lisps indecisively
from your open drawer.

You stretch like a gymnast,
ease out of your hairy jumper,
sigh like a cinder,
rest your chin on your palm.

When the phone purrs,
you pluck it reluctantly,
cross your thighs under your tweed skirt,
inspect a fingernail, recite a ritual.

In the corner of the office,
your coat submits
on tiptoe to the kiss
of the tall stand it embraces....

ATOMIC

I

Years apart and tonight Sylvie
as our lamplit faces study for idiotic degrees
very disarmingly you photo-smile to me
in your bikini, hands on knees

I realise I am not Japanese
and cannot be cataclysmic as you love
but in general the difficulty we encounter
is in controlling the fusion

II

Some like it hot
and I am condemned to die
by Marilyn's touch
her amber cloud kiss

Aye Marilyn, hands on knees, your dress
butterflies, swells aloft behind you,
and you smile so enhancingly
I am almost myself again

III

This is a dangerous year?
Oh that is wild.
In the deserted stadium at Nuremberg,
a dynamite baton, fuse of a long marathon

hotly, wetly, tingles its last trotter's
angelic grip, blazing homeward
up the last tired steps
to something Olympic

REVENUE

Sunday

Where high brushed clouds
ramble past a clovered meadow,
portly bumble-bees
flirt with daisies,
compost fumes languidly,
and lone dust occupies
a corridor skirting.

In a bare schoolroom, one girl,
resigned to her cello, hears
neither the leaves' heckling,
nor the arguing weir,
only a tennis score
commanding a sky's blues
on love, and dues.

Change

By a blonde canal bank
an exhausted drunkard
falls on a deadly edge.
Their sole coin spent,
clouds lose all shyness
and every torn shred
tells how money bled.

What was a bakery window
faintly begins to glow.
High-stacked ingots.
If naked branches
speak of finance,
last leaf notes will let go,
then wend, worthlessly.

RACHEL'S PARTY

Boughs branch barely over green canal water.
An old General, the poppy-red sun
adjusts his monocle and retires.
It is December in Baggot Street.

Snow shifts dimly pathward.
A dead gull winces, threatens
whirled white asterisks
with a stiff little fist.

Outside a hoarded shop, tattered posters
slap each other in shoulderly hilarity.
Summer is a memory of pillow scuffles,
little white feathers.

Her birthday cake glistens
like the Snow-Queen's diadem.
Candles stand in snow,
disenchanted carol singers.

Take a big breath Rachel
and swoosh them all away.
The knife cracks almond and ice.
A neat earth slice.

Speared sausages, bubbling drinks.
Tart-pools, bloodily still.
The room is a feastful
of firework light, tinsel weeds.

A cardboard box in the corner
is branded with *Added Value*.
Ribboned girls delve for discs.
Jellies also giggle.

Pale corpses sprawl on satin cushions,
yawning like carol singers.
Grins clutch their glasses.
Hands Up, Baby, Hands Up....

Martin and Rachel titter over their glasses
of spirit the colour of candleflame:
Their fingers fidget actively,
finally detecting one another....

In amber glow, cobra lamps perform.
The path is sabre-bright
and dangerous. Fragrance
of ladies lingers hereabouts.

An iced swissroll of carpet.
Last summer, woodlice mingled there,
each a toiling galley.
A moon-mint flirts behind veils.

Harry ignites the gas-ring's blue cupola
and muses on *Moskva*, a troika
in blizzard. Tea steam.
He undresses for bed

and the Siberian Express
tracks through pine forests,
advising to smother her.
Last embers dwindle, disintegrate.

More snow shifts dimly pathward.
A dead gull winces, threatens
whirled white asterisks
with a stiff little fist.

PESTILENCE: 16 JUNE 1982

The scabbed elm
gnawed by a beetle
invisibly small
will never hence
hoist leaf-pennants
blueward

The shadowy
footpath fretwork
between lawns
mirthful
this June day
will fade
too

Decay within
Cell millions rotten

fin amour
a discarded apple core

and I am a handful of skull
for some Hamlet to handle

SCENTS

Eva Braun

arm in arm at midnight
the beerhalls closed
we stroll between oaks
sit on his coat
and I rub his hair
he loves my flat shoes
my smirk

SALT

I gave you all,
and the amber fog fumes
of your city
polluted my ozone.
Now drunk and alone,
I, if anyone,
know joy, and pity.

Memory now, this hall,
these empty rooms.
I was not overstrict.
It was you,
babushka, who
decided to
escalate the conflict.

Pretty Baby

Unwanted weed within,
a frogheart for the bin.
Listening to your shoulder,
will you ever hear her?

Out, week-old star:
become gold in a jar.
Butt, glow no more:
close the furnace door.

THE PHOTOS FROM GREECE

Seen sunlit, they glitter their hues:
unsifted golden grains, a marine tear,
and a thin jet-trail chalkscoring azure,
an ever-taut birthcord that calmly waits

the snipping scissors of the sister Fates.
More fresh chalkpieces lie fragmented. Ruins.
Statues study intently their lopped limbs.
Two wrestlers struggle to escape from marble.

Behind museum glass lie a Spartan spear,
no longer flung by greasy fingers,
a Thracian helmet, no more to be tossed
off by a battle-weary soldier,

a vial for poison, emptied of venom.
At a midnight barbecue, fireworks
gesticulate to the islands below.
Meat sizzles and turns. Hands in tight pockets,

three girls giggle, and their moustached
male friends smile very whitely.
Everybody is drunk and that is why
they are smiling so happily.

Noonday heat, a narrow shady street.
A potter dozes, his muddy fingers restful.
On dry stall shelves, ever-silent armies,
ever-quiet columns, dust-shouldered urns.

THE MEANING OF THE WORD 'HUNGER'

I

The hummingbird
with shoulders twitching
gathers its many brown cloaks
into a businesslike blur
when it delicately inserts
its pointed bill
into an orchid's pink
vision of ecstasy;
though its head stays still,
its eyes may blink.

II

The vultures drift
like ashes
of burnt paper
distantly
high on their
thermal
effortlessly
fringing the air
waiting for the lions
to finish with that
red zebra.

LOWER KIMMAGE ROAD

I

A dreary afternoon.
Smithwicks People smile
at the wet footpath
where cheeky children haggle
and hang from the go-car
which, stubbornly, squeakily,
she mows towards
a washeteria door.

She strokes her peroxide curls,
ignites a cigarette, agitatedly.
The washing machine
turns its stomach.
Her husband sweats
beneath a rusting car.
At home, ketchup-smeared plates
queue to be washed.

II

Brittle twigs, stark thorns, bloodberries.
All that I would love to deny.
All joy once gulped,
now glumly thirsted for again.

All old desires warmly instilled
surreptitiously flooding each vein
if a bruised vault's snow-wisps
drunkenly descend to woo cold slates.

Brittle twigs, stark thorns, bloodberries.
All my home you have robed in
vestments clean as hospital linen.
Still, your arms open to me.

LUCIFER

White as Cleopatra's milk,
white as a new-washed toga,
the Forum's marble,
vainly streaked with Caesar's blood.

White as the whitewashed farmhouse
where, in a lamplit straw-floored kitchen,
leant over maps in dull despair,
a bicorned head is fever-browed.

White as the slopes of Berchtesgaden,
where, between negotiations,
black folded arms unfold,
and embrace alpine odours.

White as June clouds above the Wehrmacht
which rumbles into the Caucasus.
Soldiers to die, summer-sleeves rolled,
laugh for a photo, now the fight has lulled.

Magnificently white, like epileptic froth,
like legs of lice, soft flesh of egg,
a dead man's eye, wherefrom retreats seaspume,
and a floating photo of a fat girl.

White as the ambulance with lumps
on the walls: thumped responses
to an ingeniously reusable exhaust.
White as the grinning driver's teeth.

White as unwritten history pages,
button mushrooms, scientists' coats,
a supertrouper fluorescence on bunker walls,
like fallen flour, like angel dust.

GOODNIGHT

Stars

Oh lightly sprinkled sugar
on a nightpool of tar.
Is it we are leaves of rust
or ants or woodlice or cockroaches,
nightcrawlers of a forest,
trundling in baroque coaches
before snow arrives silently
as dropped leaflets, and we
duly drift
in rivers silver as ashdust?

Each eye, however solitary,
sees precision in embroidery.
We are crumbs fallen quietly
from some tall table.
We walk on broken glass.
We need no lamp.
Billion-year-old light
links to us too pin-brightly.
Oh lightly sprinkled sugar
on a nightpool of tar.

Mooney

You are smiling so beautifully at me
I don't know what I am going to do.
Have you any suggestions?
I will write them down on a petal
and float it down the stream.
The stream flows under the graveyard,
the petal is enjoying itself.
So are you, quite clearly.
Perhaps that is why you smile.

AMBER

for Carol Duffy

Have a look at this picture. Note carefully
how the sky becomes slowly stung by stars.
Warm to watch patiently the jewellery
shop clock point out how differently

the night will end for various faces:
a matter of playing pool (balls on a green
table), drinking until you're sick, and aye,
for some together to walk by, of all places,

an egg-packing factory, a church, a cinema,
she, wearing her Loreto school skirt,
he, rednosed, in a blue woollen hat,
conclude with a scene of fallen leaves.

One of two was wanting to spill the sugar.
Blame, if you wish, the adolescent
who continually was longing for her
to hurry up, each moment to be a memory,

preserved, diaried, labelled correctly,
or otherwise assert the debutant
too eager to discard his number one,
and so receive his due desert.

TROIS

Sailing to Le Havre

Lacework seaspray decks me wetly:
and almost drunk on champagne froth
I eye stern gulls drop where wake waves
throw up their can-can frills.

La Défense

In gloomy midday light
a high hoarding poster site
and a delicate drizzle are busy

overseeing the canal's stagnancy
while tower-block washing lines
like weeds waver unceasingly.

Newspapers continue to be bought
from corner stands by huddled collars
who wear out their only existence

under a clear washed sky
and even here wet poppies belie
the myth that concrete dust

makes everything miserable,
that the city is ugly,
that rain brings only rust.

Variation

What numbs my mind
constantly is the dream
where I hold her to find,
hating being my theme,
she says calmly "What was our
        warm milk is
        cold and sour...."

Heart

clenching and unclenching
sending its silent spies
to distant parts of decaying empire
hunting for words of treachery

listening like an old ocean
within which shoals collide
before being netted, as soldiers round
up dukes and kings who dared raise arms

and bring them to punishment cells
before orders are given for
their execution, the beaten drum
ignites into its hot rhythm

Fire

Always engaged to the instant,
anxious to be brilliant,
experiencing the sure thrill
of itself, giving glimpses of gold.

Digesting its rock cakes of coal,
spitting, licking its lips,
bestowing its benedictions, bowing,
scraping, growing its own roses.

A wriggling escapologist,
a clown, doing the tango with itself,
a cheeky child jacking itself
up to see what's going on....

GAULOISE

She said she would
permit no branch
of Philosophy to say
what significance should
fume from a word.
Yet the word was hers
entirely.

It was the word's
scented ashes
allowed us apart
to grow together,
wreathed fragrances,
upward-twisting
carelessly.

A tree and its ivy.
Dublin. Trinity.
Snow blossoms die
continually
where once a pair
could laugh or cry.
A dog chases a leaf,
mindlessly.

TAXMAN

for Dennis O'Driscoll

Someone has sneakily taken
my last shilling of meaning.
Here among mates, careworn as love,
a grey old coin, I slide greasily.

A watchman,
I stared into the little hellflames
dancing their hectic fandangos
till I too began to burn.

There died a screaming heretic
and the old red-faced alcoholic
grinned stupidly
at each degenerate future me.

My face hardened to a permanent papal smile.
My lips healed up completely.
It is a slow return from the furnace.
Out of the ash-heap a beetle marches.

The Gospel says
to give God what is his and never
tells me why the same faces appear
more worn in each new year.

I only ask to be permitted to retain
a token of what once was me,
what will remain unwritten.
Sir, teach me to gleam again.

OPIA

Daybreak

Clear stab hauled was I down
Down stab clear hauled I was
Hauled I stab was clear down
Was I stab clear hauled down
Clear was I stab hauled down
Stab down hauled was I clear

Mistress

They're everywhere this time of year
on building site
in country roadside ditches
beside drooping nettles
wasteland polka dots
dwarves' handkerchieves
little firing range flags
pouting red lips

They're an obsession
le rouge et le rouge
prostitute's make-up
let me inhale you
let me be drunk on you
let's be vampires

Carry my corpse Valkyrie
Mats said with clenched teeth
let me hear
instead of Wagnerian celibacy
Use your wanking finger
to wag me a warning
Like Lennon
sing Please Please Me

Republic

Cool ceaseless blue:
the branches are chirrupy aviaries
where sycamores generously
unclench fistfuls of leaves

Arthritic knuckles,
twigs finger the March air,
begin to bud

Little diamonds decorate
the leaves of grass
A fat jogger pants past

Footpath dust sweeps itself.
Major, Cadbury's Flake,
Ireland's Only Quality Sunday.
The Dodder swallows thirstily
where a weed-garlanded
rusted shopping trolley
lies like a dead fly

The scene is engoldened.
A bus-stop's squashed *Bruscar* can lies
like dropped knickers about its ankles

A silver Datsun Violet
has tried to kiss a bollard
and weeps like a rejected lover.
The seats bow towards Mecca.

This is Ireland of the wink and the nod
the green notes in the tightfisted wad
the nixer the Guinness the Gardai
Parish Priest and JCB
Today Tonight and CIE

[*JCB*: shovel-tractor. *CIE*: Córas Iompair Éireann,
Irish Transport Company.]

Romantic Period

When the woman leaves,
she may not have died,
but she is dead to you,
and it is too easy to re-slit
the wound in longing to sip
again the reddest wine.

A Walk in the Park

On a sunbathing day
all skins turn to scarlet
and any nurse who disagrees
will receive eyes
like bleeding poppies
and become a Solidarity banner
in a Renault 5's rear seat.

Norn Arln

a wee folla know was kilt
stone dad by there you see
on Bolfost today he wasn't
onvolved if you know whaddamean
jus walkin along this side
the road one day opened fair
withight onny warn atoll
then they wonder whey the
weewons throw stones adam
bleedin bostards

TOP OF THE POPS

Drimnagh

Trolleys full of *Pampers* and *Thrift* biscuits,
fat women queue. There's the local TD's clinic.
Leave me sterile if I am rid of this septic.
Deliver me from *Pam's Boutique*s and *Disk-It*s.

Oil-haired men smoke, swop tips, and spit.
One wears a leather jacket, reads the *Mirror*.
Bluely adorning a footpath beside dogshit
winks a windscreen's millionth losing tear.

However often the Sweep is held, you cannot win,
being already dead. Now flies fuck on you,
decaying dog. When your last bark was due,
you still blindly eyed some rusted dustbin.

You lived with your nose. You weren't rare.
Now you can't sniff yourself. You stink the air.

Charmer

Hair darkly silken that had seemed exotic
fronded green eyepools, unliveable in.
The smile was too amiable. Too reptilian.
Leave, little woman. I am sick of your music.

So moving a tail-end. Well held within
jeans tight as snakeskin, she'd be breathless.
Sometimes seal-moist, she'd hiss when breathing in.
A dancefloor's her home; no zoo's as odorous.

Lizard-lady, be natural, don't seem so shy.
Your tongue darts poor flies, giving death's kiss.
You are no more than your clothes, dear miss.
Don't come biting me and expect no reply.

Your blood is cold, unflowing, like lard.
I kick chameleons. I kick them hard.

Cell

I'm back doing solitary. Private hell
of a bedroom englooms a failed romance.
I didn't even get to see you dance.
Eurythmic bullets. Now they'd be helpful.

It was you who got me out, former informer.
It's hard to escape from the maze a mind
can twist itself into. I did, to find
you were more than one man's bedwarmer.

It's the boredom kills. Not the screw's frown.
How like you this? I stare at a cold floor.
Await the scratch of a key in the door.
Raise my head to see you looking down.

Your visits irritate, deceptive elf.
Depart. Evaporate. Go fuck yourself.

Cup

A first and final night. Wet as the piper's rats
we saw Heffo's Army gather like worse weather,
waving their scarves and sodden paper hats.
We were celebrating being together.

On Exchequer Street, a cup spilled soft rain.
And I always supported you. You said that I was daft.
I had meant the Offaly replay. Last winter's campaign.
You wore white and blue. I wore maroon. We laughed.

And all my surroundings told me I'd lose.
The conversations about us were so banal.
Mingling feline lusts, we crossed the canal,
sipped tea, were two. *Up the Hill. More booze.*

The Jacks are back. We're the boys in blue.
We'll hammer these culchies. Show them who's who.

Computer

A list is what it spews when it feels blue.
A dull diet of digits, hard to digest.
All Monday I process an ancient list
of printed names. Only a pen to chew.

Didn't know you kept one yourself.
Annotating every nightclub conquest.
Ensuring that there's none you've missed.
Replacing it on your perfume's proud shelf.

Silk sang the essence of the web you wove.
Glad to have made it into your pop-chart,
reaching number one for a week, like *Start*,
Open Your Heart, or your tongue's *Tainted Love*.

May my name thereon luminously every night
hound your needed sleep, dissolve spite.

40

Diamonds

Restful on velvet behind large windows,
they wink to tall and small couples who walk
hand in hand. Of the ecstatic girls' glow,
of rainbows' broken light, they cannot talk.

Though individual, each rarity
lies with the soft bent light it would imbue
in us; theirs is a borrowed clarity.
They entomb light as an emblem of two.

Faces surround each cold core's flaw:
though exposed, they, untorn, unbruised, uncut,
say the dove's coat is that of the jackdaw.
Lent light, these substances are only soot.

Hard eyes, whisperers of facts, stark and bare,
they talk of care, and learning not to care.

THREE TREES

for Sylvie

What has Morality to do
with the forest of hands
a schoolmistress calmly commands?
What puerile philosophy bends,
a well-thrashed tree, to you,
and craves your love's good glue?

Is it the tree *Infection*
whose skin, crusted, crumbly,
is mined by multifarious insects?
Green is aerosolled on its trunk.
Penknives have nicked hearts
deep into its bark. Mongrels
have solemnly pissed against it.

Is it the tree *Conviction*
who lives alone, contorted, wronged?
This tree is a pair of handcuffed hands:
one clutches tightly at earth,
refusing to release it;
the other opens generously.

Is it the tree *Adoration*
that rose while you were away?
She is not popular with the others.
She has a weird hairdo.
She behaves eccentrically.
You may like her. You may not.

Her leaves are your fans.
They all anxiously want to
shake hands with you.
Half-weeping, half-smiling,
they tremble now you're here.
They bring you bouquets.
They will clap whatever you say.

SEINE SONNETS

Abbesses

Braking beneath the brow of Sacré Coeur
I stooped from a taxi and climbed, burdened,
a varnished crooked stair, to kiss a friend.
Dear Florence, I remember your sisterly care.

We pass red bricks of St Jean de Montmartre
and I relive the masses' frail incense,
streetscapes that were her hurtful absence.
The café's not the same without Pierre: Sartre.

Too sensitive we two. Explosive, delicate.
We share too much, particularly sense.
Cloistered, we have our vows of silence.
A lift fountains us up to meet Arlette

and hear *Carmen*. "La fleur de la cigarière...."
We smile politely, each itching on our chair.

Choisy-le-Roi

Then or now, the Seine could have been the Styx.
The sun glared furnace-red through stubborn haze
that had draped the city for several days.
The molten river shoved past Monoprix.

A sordid wind ripped wickedly. And I too ran.
It boasted of its achievements, it blustered.
It pecked, and worried waves became flustered.
It delivered dust to Rue Camille Desmoulins.

Bronze leaves flipped wildly on every bended tree.
Your door did not open to your greatest fan.
The letter-box said silverly: Constantinou-Despatin.
From all directions, wind walloped, caned me.

I stepped down to the Metro's underworld,
once flighty flag, now tightly furled.

Les Halles

The phone demands insistently a ring, a ring.
The Celtic harp that once you plucked in me
is buried deeper than anything under Wood Quay.
Ten special fingers that had me humming

that Schubert trio in E flat major
demolished on sacred ground our relation,
burying it for future excavation.
Those gold girders, like me, will be sager.

The same varnished boards will still gleam.
You'll yawn on the creaking wicker chair.
Only a mattress for a bed. The same air
will haunt strangely again. And we will seem

awkward characters in a Beckett play,
the stage too bare, not knowing what to say.

44

Louvre

The shuttered houses heaped on top of one
another are eyelids that drowsily wake.
They're here not for my but for your sake.
The mystified city is touched pinkly by sun.

A tricolour flagellates itself above the Louvre.
Mona Lisa smiles tiredly at each twitchy lens
and exiting, hands in pockets (defence
against thieves), I watch your bum manoeuvre.

Venus de Milo looks down, calmly neutral,
at Japs, Yanks, and Huns in their hordes.
Grinning negroes are selling clockwork birds
where Napoleon walked. The sky is gunmetal.

Windows wide, well fed, we inhale late news.
Pigeons scuffle for ledge places, like kicked-off shoes.

Come

and do not delay. Be my loaves of rationed bread.
Curb the artillery's repetitive dull curse
that daily has me need you, my field tent nurse.
Bandage well this wounded heavy head.

I would read you not cookery manuals nor
the *Don Giovanni* score whose 'Il mio tesoro'
now warms this empty room. Yes. OK. Tomorrow.
In a train we'll end this four-year war.

Then you'll hear the house regularly shudder
with the Metro's muffled celebratory thunder.
Fireworks will crack ecstatically, fall asunder.
We will whisper rude secrets to each other.

Wear your red beret and the woollen dress.
The Aran one. The one with easy access.

Kathy

"And what do you do?" I asked the punk girl
upon whom hung a badly torn tee-shirt
and the minutest patent leather skirt.
"Oh, I'm a photograph," fingering a curl

she casually replied. Then the tendril
deftly unwound itself, fell into line.
She shows me her photos and I blindly incline
to view garbage, squat houses, a full till,

spattered fake blood, grimaces of false agony
on faces of hatcheted punks in Berlin.
Two nuns insert a huge statue of the virgin
into a Fiat 127. "Aren't they funny?

You must meet Hans...." We walk to where he waits.
I notice he is wearing roller skates.

The Sylvia

There was a storm. Blue light cracks seized
greasy mast tips, illumining the dark.
I thought perhaps we were being teased,
each of us, each unsuccessful spark.

I knew it was a pirate ship because
I saw the muscling skull-and-crossbones flag
being hoisted slowly next day, until it was
surrounded by hoarse gulls that watched it wag.

The sailors were like large spiders from hell
in their rigged webs. Their only catch, a gull,
I didn't see until the sheets began to swell.
His feathered brains reddened her hull.

The ship shuddered when the cannons' harsh boom
made other sails shiver, seeing us loom.

Gull

The moon was a bloodshot eye, unable to peep,
and then it became a golden token,
a Spanish coin that blinks when woken
from five centuries of deep seabed sleep.

There was a buccaneer, he wanted me
badly. I was wet with fear when he stuck
his bright cutlass in the stern saying "Let's fuck."
So I gave in, and we moved with the sea.

His face knew I loved what he was wearing,
a blue and white sweat-smelling sailor shirt.
He kept pumping so strongly beneath my skirt
I thought I'd bleed to death with the tearing.

I must have passed out. Later, when I woke
on the deck's salt, I heard a lone gull croak.

St Michel

Outside, construction starts again. A saw
coughs, splutters and whines. *Undercover*
is the radio's order to every late lover.
I'm fascinated by one wide open jaw.

But you have work to do. We're roped with rules.
"Fuck all rules." Yes. Such truant talk incites
me to recall last night's cobbled bridge, Seine lights,
Laurel and Hardy, two drunken tottery fools

singing *Dominique*. If a man has not a God he makes
one for himself. True. I love the smell of Metro.
Me too. But I cannot stomach your *A bientôt*.
Then, innards wrestle, like a nest of snakes

spitting at each other. I despise the bell
that shoves doors between us, at St Michel.

Oui

When sick of cash prizes on dull quiz shows,
or taunted by those adolescent stars,
affronted by this city's neon glows,
hoarded derelict sites, cold burnt-out cars,

I hesitantly follow this old nose
to places where weeds rise beside bright bars
and inhale from the illusory rose,
hopelessly. I still need taint-free attars.

So, readily confessing it's a thrill
to hold you again, beautiful gypsy,
I must say we've become briefly derailed.

Did Christian denial cause this? When will
making new love be no chosen inanity,
no tired exchanging of masks? Have we failed?

Amoureuse

I noticed everyone was dressed in red.
I, not they, had committed a cardinal sin.
Were I now to confess my evil within,
my cleansed soul with God would be re-wed.

They didn't like my short black hair,
what I said about their odour of sin,
how faces deceive, that my own heaven
was to be able to love them in prayer.

All I could say reversed their leaden law.
Told to repent, I was given a crucifix.
When I refused to join those heretics
I was surrounded by piles of fresh straw.

So I felt nothing when the last priest turned
and walked away, because I'd always burned.

Drumcliff

Remember our wet August in Sligo?
Why did we ever want to overplease
with the notion of "Where you go, I go"?
My dear woman. We were not born gypsies.

The sun's appearances were rather rare.
When he did come, it was to accept
offerings of steam that rose in prayer,
a silver wealth, taken from trees that wept.

Balisodare was breathing its cleansed air
when the tent crowds left their broken Guinness
bottles. The rain had eased. Was it not there,
tell me, O my abandoned tearful Tess,

you said you'd love to hear *Leaving Nancy*?
Never before, never again, such constancy.

Tear

Once wombed, I must have sighed *Tu es Française?*
I, drip, in my madness, dared not defy
you. I who once did safely occupy
a corner of your eye, was kissed away.

Swept here to the Atlantic's floor
with my million sisters and brothers.
We all sway, your fanatical supporters.
Even in Normandy, you hear our roar.

Listen, you said you'd love to live alone.
I've been through it. Brimming on your cheek
I magnified in you what was most weak,
and was wiped clean, finished, done.

It was my function to be perfectly formed.
When what I really wanted was your warmth.

High

Some things demand that they be taken more
of, pretending to give ease. Such a scent
I found, though slowly, headachingly, your
presence dear, a much-craved intoxicant.

I would have drunk dry the source of that spring,
my head enfumed by its unique clear call,
in our love game I'd have staked everything,
if, loose-limbed rag-doll, you'd let me freefall

to you again. If now after I've wheezed
until a city's beneath me, I'm one hour
remotely in danger of being pleased,
it's not because I'm on old Eiffel's tower,

having my face slapped by wind that numbs;
it's that you're here, high scatterer of crumbs.

Shakespeare

I let the liquid lubricate my throat,
as words, *du vin rosé*, often do. The soup
is slurpable, and I'm Roderigo, my coat
is that of a gulled gentleman, a dupe.

I hold the flaking bread and break it up,
freeing a small white fleet of Turkish boats
on the Pontic in this storm-free, dull cup.
Nothing, *rien du tout*. The sick clock gloats.

Is love only love when it's without hope?
You came, bright-eyed, and professionally kissed
my moorish ear, the cold ear of an eager dope,
pouring poison there. I was Cassio then, pissed.

I lower my wounded head, stiff with loss,
to bloodied sheets, a moon-cool brow, wet moss.

Les Fleurs du Mal

I dreamed I saw the fickle flowers grow,
the matador twitchings, each one a red
ascension, coolly lost in itself, a slow
unclenching of a fist, a fist that bled.

I dreamed I heard the gasping dying radio:
Take Cover, Take Cover was being repeated
and each city, when dealt its facial blow,
was a boxer, raising its ugly head.

Each flower was a dawn, inkling grey,
then heart-breaking lapse of luxuriant light,
purple and blue and orange, a strange rash

evaporating fish and boats and bridge and bay,
painting a perplexed world with stings of white
where fickle flowers sucked, on stalks of ash.

THREE PAINTINGS

I

Salvador Dali: *The Average Bureaucrat*, 1930

Memoland is mostly desert, and very dry.
Here is one of its huge inhabitants,
surveying us with his sour eye,
that cannot blink at words like *Love*:
in such stale heat, no one has ever
learned to dance. They're too heavy.
They don't even bother to try.
The snail's moist brain perpetually kisses
its own fragile security; only a giant's foot
will break his home, his brittle back,
and ignorantly end the work of years.

Bronze-shouldered and indifferent
to the copper rocks, unworked of ore,
he affects a bulb-blank honesty.
Sometimes his eyebrows, nose
and moustache may slide down to his throat
to snooze blissfully in siesta there,
a contemplative Mexican, lost in the light
of his own large lungs, their hot air.
One day, he'll drop an empty bucket
into a well he'll bore; and his
face will shed itself completely.

II
Pierre-Auguste Renoir: *Le Moulin de la Galette*, 1876

Don't talk of the loveliness of the latest hat,
or what the trees are clearly reaching towards;
don't talk about the shaken chandeliers, things that
hang too delicately: there is no time for cards.
Let the music's rhythm sway your auburn hair:
away, away; your drinks will still be there.

Dance, because the given light is clinging
too fretfully, and it will only last a while:
dance, find a man's heart, listen to it singing;
no note-taking at the table. Yet still smile
to us out here so unaffectedly,
and still ignore the man we'll never see.

III

Claude Monet: *Les Coquelicots*, 1873

Descending the slight spilling slope
are two black-ribboned white-hatted ladies.
Darkly dressed, facelessly as Faith or Hope,
they both proceed with grand light ease.
They're going somewhere directly ahead;
we're led to think it's blotched with red.

Full warmness won't come until midday.
Only the little boy has a face, and he's
shoulder-deep, clutching his scarlet spray.
All's quiet beneath; ants feel for rhapsodies.
Though good for gathering invisible pollen,
such long skirts are not for strolling fields in.

Her parasol cannot be for rain or sun,
it's just to hold, like the imaginary
rail she steadily grips. But what weapon
has fallen from the hand we're so wary
of? What senate, should she sneeze suddenly,
will be red-robed enough to say she's guilty?

Behind uninterested trees, the world's still
there, real, like the half-hidden home, happy
in its flesh-pink slates, its three sills
seeing distantly, differently, all we see:
scarecrow figures ignoring wide-beaked weeds,
a creaking vessel, a frame that bleeds.

The distorted tree that crookedly oversees
has almost a head and has almost
ushered these people and all of these poppies
to our side of the field. Is it a ghost?
If we wait for the other ever-coming pair,
will we breathe fresh or fumy air?

ROMANCE

after Alexander Blok

I

Like wind, the music of spring
arriving from another country.
It seems someone's dug a hole
in the sky, and found a hoard of gold.

Perhaps it is a bottomless well,
the very source of this spring evening....
Red-face, remembering winter's thunder,
dreaming like any other angry star.

And equally sombre, equally deep
strings are stroked somewhere in me,
by wind, the music of spring,
arriving from another country.

II

Remember when we found
the town, wrapped in its rain?
Wet, lost for words, we walked,
loving each brown puddle.

Later, the moon hiked herself up
high over the town's dark wall....
Were we on a wrong road?
We wouldn't have gone back.

Maybe our love was rain, or mist,
perhaps the puddles had no purpose....
But those dripping drops, I'm sure,
mixed with something in me.

III

Look how the snow has drifted
where we walked last night:
the rose-hint mild
morning lifts up its light.

Look at the scarlet streaks
pinking the snow,
the beach all washed,
brazen, aglow.

Melting ice moves,
adds itself to a stream;
and my girl is like snow,
unreal, a dream.

IV

You left me wearing red,
like the rippling circles made by
imagined splash of sun. I still hear
your fading footsteps in my mind.

You could be in the next street....
Or are you up to your waist in heather?
How do you expect me to live
in a silence that is your absence?

Your footsteps are growing louder,
falling on floorboards in my empty skull:
girl in poppyflame hue, why
traipse in circles, eternally?

V

Alone beneath the same few stars,
the same black blanket full of holes,
with people everywhere howling
about food and money.

Alone, hearing such roars,
seeing a different world,
yet remaining two-faced,
pretending to see theirs.

Or wrapping a parcel for her,
thinking of her next perfumed letter,
letting your ear do the waiting,
dying for those scrawled words.

Even the little heart
of a gull, far from its wave-splashed cliff,
calls out familiarly
to its nest-bound mate, and is heard.

VI

Another autumn day dies:
a yellow leaf spins aimlessly.
Light's fresh, air's clean,
yet everything seems worn.

Each day the world grows old,
each year a yellow leaf falls off:
and we remember, or like to think, that
autumn was never sad, when we were young.

VII

My mind is a dark church
where my poor words help me relax.
I wait for a beautiful lady
and inhale smells of wax.

In the shadow of a column,
I hear a creaking door.
But it's not her, it's only a statue
of the lady who's made me sore.

I wanted the woman, not her image,
I wanted her to be a faithful wife....
But from cornices high above,
angels smirk at my miserable life.

Love, quiescent, like a candle,
my wish is to drip down your face, a tear;
lost in silence, lost for a word,
I think I've found you here.

VIII

Forgotten graves, lost headstones, grass.
Forgotten words, whispers, stillness.
Love-breath, re-pulse in me....
Carry blossoms in my bloodstream this spring.

Forgotten graves, where I once breathed
like the wind, adolescent rhymes
of love to you. Where you breathed life
on my face, like grass on lost headstones.

A WALK ON A WINTER'S DAY

after Wang Wei

Wilfrid Road

The balding rust-haired man smiles.
He has just sold his car.

The bald-tyred rusting car smiles.
He has just lost a cruel master.

Rathmines Shopping Centre

Magazine faces smile,
begging to be bought.

An orange-mouthed young girl
flicks away her ice-pop stick.

Tomatoes, celery and lettuce
are richly displayed for the hungry:

but the poor red-brown loinchop
shows only its solitary gleaming blood-drop.

Upper Rathmines Road

Dandelions no longer crowd the derelict site.
Delicate seeds no longer float off to anywhere.

Red and white oildrums line the centre of the road.
Polythene tape flimsily links them.

The excavator's asleep, but the circling gulls
keep begging it to wake:

and here are rows of robed queens,
curlered heads attended, reading glossy magazines.

The showroom's new cars are saddest of all.
The sun teases them, but they're not let out to play.

Villiers Road

This is the door
she pushed open and shut
a thousand times.

Here are the footpath cracks
her low heels
wore.

This moss lodged between red bricks
saw her leaving early for work,
head high.

This moss lodged between red bricks
saw her coming home late
with Chinese food, head low.

Frankfort Avenue

It's always Je suis desolé,
feeling like a house for sale....

The granite sill will be warm next summer
for a new bikini'd bottom.

Kenilworth Square

On their pillars two stone lions yawn

A woman is washing her door step

She wrings her orange cloth, hearing it drip

As if tickled, the tall tree shakes childishly

But there are no leaves left to fall

ADOLESCENT MORNINGS

I

The turned tractor begins its calm new incision.
By ears of black and white delinquent cows,
flies disport themselves, doing the twist
to the tractor's rocking and rolling.
Shiny grass gallops off to nowhere,
then abruptly turns around, and madly
whipped on, takes up its new direction.
The fields writhe: pus greenly bleeds;
a steel-blue blade tosses up wilted weeds.

II

A rag-wrapped crowd of crows arrives
and raucously begins to laugh
at the tattered crucifixion
who's pleading to be left alone.
A fox stops, attends the breeze,
continues, sniffs a stone, as
the rain's tittering ceases.
Driven from lakes, bowed rushes, reeds:
behind abandoned cones, a hedgehog feeds.

III

When the blackbird's flute solo begins,
the air is strangely eastern:
a smiling caliph-sun arrives;
advised by ear-whispering courtier-clouds,
he accepts the trees' tribute, kissed
cups, pools of liquid gold,
embroidered veils of silver mist.
Fledgling leaves grasp at nests, their needs:
breaking open, fathers' yielding fists, seeds.

THE MEANING OF THE WORD 'TREE'

No more ashamedly attempt to woo
ungrateful crows, or parade in proud park;
the fields will not choreograph for you
the anxiousness of red, the dimming dark.

You wasted your thin talent. There are few
of you left to listen to wakened lark
saying it doesn't know what it should do,
estates' dawn dogs, their unrepentant bark.

You went one night in a fulsome rich gust;
unprettily falling over yourself, you paled,
and everyone thought you'd only fainted.

But you were dead. Somehow you'd lost your lust
to live. Knowing idiots said you'd failed
in your purpose, which was to be tainted.

I'M GLAD YOU ASKED THAT QUESTION

These are the motionless antipathies,
the spewed-on cliff, the flagrant apple trees,
the sullen shoulder-hiding dove,
french-kissing snakes, unanxious in their love.

Look at the groping grass, distilled green lust,
the never-satisfied carousing dust,
hanging spiders, and all the silly little things
with barely adequately glazed wings.

Look at the demon hiding in the waterflea's
heart, beating the walls, uttering low pleas;
the hermit-crab building a home the tide
destroys daily; he has nowhere to hide.

Look at the aphids on their swaying poppystems,
the tramps in the park coughing up their phlegms,
the ants, like stockbrokers doing their deals,
all businessmen, with no time for their meals.

Look at the entangling ivy, choking the disused mill,
the million fleeing hearts, the shoal of brill,
the spewed-on cliff, the flagrant apple trees;
these are the motionless antipathies.

RELIEF

A pestilent gall to me... KING LEAR I.iv

Strand

A jet scratches the sky,
the beach wrinkles its forehead,
the sea-weed wipes its lips,
a crab embraces air, beckons. Shy
fringes rise and crash, wed
briefly, disintegrate in drips.

Rain

Colours ran away from cigarette packets,
matches were canoes and butts were barrels
in the little rapids that galloped
in the gutters; kerbs were sheer cliff faces.
Sediment, silt, rilled, gathered, grew.

The streetlamps tried to preserve
their dignity, but even they, by six,
were quivering redly, and cars at that rush
hour smoked sullenly. Longer lasting tyres
lasted a little longer; TV aerials whistled.

Suddenly, ninety-nine diminutive orblets
flung themselves in several final leaping
waves against a door in Longwood Avenue,
knocking where no hall bulb shone.
But that didn't mean there wasn't one.

St Patrick's Day

A majorette's spinning silver stick
was high over slowly moving lorries
laden with little lawns and streaming
ribbons, long tongues trying to lick
the wind dry. Frowned with worries,
foreheads of tin-whistlers were teeming.

Schubert

No one tries hard as trees
to love: each grows its own way,
each finding its own ease,
each designs its own day....
Think of the Trout Quintet,
Steyr, summer trees over a river
dappled with bloodspots,
leaves freckling exquisitely....

Midsummer

The afternoon sky is saying nothing.
The windows are all open, the air
is standing to attention. A bluebottle
has just bashed his head against the glass,
recovered, and flown dazedly out.
The swing next door is creaking.
A jet goes slowly over.

Lilac flowers are positioned along
the path-edge, swinging in the sunshine.
From behind swayed leaves, bird-natter,
argumentative perhaps, arrives.
The lawn is toast-throated, the big-eyed
daisies by the ivy wall are preening themselves,
the fridge is giving itself a good shake.

A door displays its
purple flakes of paint,
an overgrown garden contains
two turned-over dustbins,
and what has spilled from them: *Woman*,
a face disfigured by tea-leaves,
gold foil-wrap of an Oxford Lunch.

Dejection

Her voice and mine converse: we discover
Hope, and other friendly characters, one
in the sense of being written by one. My lady
is not found in mirrors, angles, aspects
or the instant of a shattered filament's
million painted pale blue indecisions.

Low, unworthy as fog, only as a lover
will she speak of absence, absence of sun:
an active well, a cave of frantic bats, a shady
insect-dizzy spot, a void, peopled with defects,
fistfuls of pine needles, where good intents,
like tears, dumbly take up their positions.

Running

As quicksilver quickens like sweat,
as leaves loosen, all hustle and bustle,
as a single swallow manipulates itself,
as a tear in the deep wound of the sea
soothes the throat of the anemone,
as parliaments of spruces congregate,
as a cathedral encloses flame-stained pillars
of air, as an altar-candle cowers,
as a road aches with dark scourge marks,
as a tree triumphs occasionally....

LOUIS

Stompin' at the Savoy

Somehow you know the lime-green lamps, the plants
that fringe the smoky dark: negro waiters in black ties
show you to your candlelit menu; your elation
steals that of the nearby roulette wheel. If you dance
to the negress's voice, you will feel your lady's
hard emerald brooch press upon your carnation.

Yet you have no hidden holster of chamois leather;
it is only you, less your slick black hair, and less
your dark pinstripe suit, who tangos with your lasting
love, your soul-love: she holds her pink headband feather,
brash, bare-shouldered, in her sequined pink dress.
The piano sparkles, and angelic brass keeps blasting.

Basin Street Blues

Today, today is a day I cannot get
over the nakedness of skin, cold sky;
the clods, the clouds that someone flings,
the earnest boilings, the intense buildings,
sea-steam, moved mist, and gulls, a grey-white few.

Late sun-streaks litter down like clarinet
notes, stabbing, owl-brightly, at twigs, the things
that stay in sight, leaves clean as angels' wings,
a hospital window's wideness. The squeak, the cry,
is there, is air: light-frail, gold-good, knot-new.

JESUS

Jesus was tired; he had been walking alone
all day. He rested beneath the shade
of an olive tree, breathing deeply
the fragrant air. Insects were busy
in the fields about him; he watched
the birds rising and trilling
in the cloud-flecked light blue.

Women were coming out of their
little white houses in the valley,
beating their mats; one woman was
dragging her boy by the ear because
he had been taunting a dog. Others,
in groups, were at their washing stones,
where the river sparkled in the valley.

Dust rose in clouds behind a column
of marching, laughing, Roman soldiers;
the rhythmic muffled sound of their
sandals soon diminished. Their tall
spears still shone in the distance
when all sound had gone. Beside his hand,
Jesus saw an ant carrying a crumb
larger than itself. The wind was warm.

CHRISTIA

I

the hammer needs
the nail

the wrists limply
give no more gestures

clouds above graveyards
disburse their downpours

the mother
understanding the core of pain

a universe's heartbeat stops
all men die

who loves
lives

II

look at the Pietà
Jesus heavily dead

mother woefully alive
both stolen from stone

MORALITY

I Will Follow

In shop windows I walk down Abbey Street,
and am urged to buy a lamp, some books, a bed.
This footpath is getting to know my feet.
The morning is: gusty, gutsy, well-fed.

Lunch is: a ham sandwich, a pint of stout,
viewing of dirty-knickered gulls on the Liffey,
the rich nectar you mustn't go without,
that sordid whorehouse choir, La Verité.

Work: moving parcels collide more or less
randomly, are opened, re-sealed. O stopped-clock
city of rained-on, pram-ensconced *Herald* or *Press*,
shifty suedeheads, slagheaps by cobbled dock,

my ego is just able to refrain
from landsliding into utter disdain.

Going Underground

When I re-ascended at Bonnes Nouvelles,
headlines spoke to me of the Lebanon
that morning, where girders collapsed and fell
on a classroom of refugee schoolchildren;

other events in the new north of Israel:
mother lifting her dead pyjama'd son
to a lorryload of corpses, an image of hell,
with fatigued Christian soldiers looking on.

Sifted rubble of what was a city
held up by excavator claws, the past
being killed for a never-arriving future good;

present, swallowed-up white cells of pity.
Beneath haranguing helicopters, Belfast,
Beirut, prattling bullets, puddles of blood.

Souvenir

Love is not love which whimpers when it's kicked
or that sort of thing. No, it is a decadence
that unfolds like flimsy red petals, flicked
out from within. It looks like wind-wrecked tents.

It is like the language heard in a pub,
behind collected pint-glasses' clinking,
it is the genie-lamp you never get to rub,
costly smoke of unillumined thinking:

"I like to walk on a Sunday, I'm a footpath-man,
I believe in going, but always coming back.
Look after number one, be your own best fan,
that's what I fuckin say. We should attack

the fuckin North." Two in a café: "Oui,
je suivrais, mais tu suivras, toi aussi...."

The Winner Takes It All

The wise-crack: "It is a milk-chocolate prick."
Or, lass to her lover: "You're really good!"
He: "Oh, I practise a lot on my own...." The wick
I've shrivelled to: corpse-smile, rat-ridden food.

Apartments erect themselves where we stood.
The wide smile that at its most ecstatic
announced heady boom-times for my hot blood
gently turns my self-pitying stomach.

Now I understand why first must be last.
In Dublin, everything is inverted: heroes
here are robust failures, we never tire

of shroud-grey sky. When we eat, we fast.
In living, we die daily. No warmth, no wild rose
freshens. Only victims are besieged by fire.

PAINTING ONESELF

Rembrandt van Rijn

I look at you
wearing neither smile nor
frown, only as a man,
fudgy, and getting old.
I paint the things I love
not what others agree
is good. And now my house is sold.

I may be through.
But I paint what I see, and for
no one but me. I have no plan,
no great method. I try to hold
a face's thought. I have nothing to prove.
I am utterly useless with money.
But I can tell dead meat from gold.

Vincent van Gogh

My head's
a café of drunken prostitutes, unborn
babies, and instruments that scrape.
Sometimes I hear music beneath it all
shaking from every leaf: *No, don't....*
World-sea in cave of ear eroding me.
I crumble and fall.

Rust-reds....
God listening through ears of corn,
in còbbled starlit streets, in fields of rape,
look down through yellow face of moon
on burnt-out brow cold as a font
and dapple sketchily
with rain, this olive tree, this stone.

THE MEANING OF THE WORD 'FLUTTER'

Zinc is up
Copper is up

the papers flutter into the air
above the varnished populated floor
and some brokers cry
and some brokers do not cry
and some bank balances are up
and some bank balances are down
but the grand total is still the same

And the arctic tern says to itself
I honestly do not belong here
it must be time to go

And the weary jumbo-jet says to itself
I despise the USA I despise the USSR
it must be time to go

And a tramp dying beneath a bridge
looked into the murky depths and thought
it must be time to go

Gold is down
Silver is down

wings, leaves, espouse the air
above the unpopulated fields
and there are no brokers
and there are some badgers
and there are no bank balances
and the word was made flesh
when the grand total could not have been the same

AIRPORTS

Dublin

Renoir's *After the Bath* on the white wall:
you towel your hair; I just fall and fall.

On you are the most precious rolling drops,
one of which, my tongue, most aptly, stops.

My garden poppies give no fume.
But you do. And the hydrangea's in bloom.

Now I do not know the meaning of more.
Still, you seem to; and you smile. So I soar.

The only winner in this parting is
a plane, property of Europe Air Services.

Charles de Gaulle

Those big lips, as if about to whistle,
were hesitant to form a new word.
A word you'd never seen before. Thistle.
"Tea Cell". I bought what I could not afford.
Your deep laugh when I say "Gare du Nord".
Your clothes are stinking heavily
of sweat and smoke, and this is beautiful.
You hold your cigarette aloft, and look at me
with eyebrows raised, quizzically.

HAROLD'S CROSS

Contain me beneath thatch and low grey walls,
where the crowd I hear's a fire, its hissing calls,
and from a small window, let me see thin spray,
white dots on a dreary midwinter day.
Let me hear the calm of sober violin,
and with rations enough, pursue wishes
abnormal, to be alone, wash old dishes,
unloose thick ropes of hate within.

Let me unlearn routine, deregister office
from memory, forget the horde of familiar faces
each day serves up, the groaning of lorries,
sad revolving doors, queues of worries.
Place me beyond the swag-bellied landlord's
stale smile, glances from girls in satin disco
gear. Put me beyond their dream, San Francisco,
their jackpot-hopes for what they can't afford.

Beyond all grinning jewel-eyed idols. And let
them see the crack they're trying to paper over
is a deep pink canyon they can never cover
up: no one is equal. Some minds aspire, others fret
their days away, doing nothing; the difference
between unmortgaged trees and the young pair who go
to them, planning forty cool summer lawns they'll mow,
is shifting among the thick leaves: Patience.

A Christmas-Eve crowd, hailed by a stone-eyed man
to repent, hears sounds empty as a Pepsi-can
echo: they are lost sheep without a way,
join with me brethren, let us pray....
Another voice, behind unheeding centuries,
from a scarred, dejected face, from two boards,
looks down in rags, with injured hands, his words
unfelt, unheard, his breath a wheeze.

BLOOD AND SOIL

Gustav Mahler: *Symphony Number One*

Walking across the field,
being berated by swifts,
copper clouds mimed my eddying
and the red whirlpool, the wish
then, was to lose her, and kiss
instead the times we wore.

Ludwig van Beethoven: *Violin Concerto*

She gave me naked stalks
for answers, and my desire
was theirs: to build her
an unswaying thing so high
it would unskilfully stab
the coldest sky.

Wolfgang Amadeus Mozart: *Requiem*

No incense, no incantation
can take the ache
or ever re-enact her eyes' activity
or unstain the gloss from her hair.
But here, here is a worthless air,
a ditch-born thing, crying for her.

RELIGION

I

And the crosses arrived.
Slowly, few at first, they
would appear like mushrooms
or sudden flowers in dark places.
Fed by beautiful coloured light,
they would smell of poison and death.

And the solitary tree
that creaked so piteously
did not believe it was father
to so many sick imitations
in weathered stone.

II

And the crosses went.
Slowly, few at first, they
would go like rising last swallows
or Easter snow from shady crevices.
Pursued by streams of golden beams,
they would smell of flowers and life.

And the surrounded tree
that stood so sternly
then believed it was a mother
being plagued by its own
sprightly offspring.

TWO

I

Does your face pain you
when your doorbell's brief song
releases you from the greasy rack
upon which your muscles daylong
tent-tautened to a cheap sky's blue?

Does your face pain you
when those night-darkened lashes
see themselves looking back
and wind damply dashes
your window's chip-shop view?

Does your face pain you
when the yawny young sun
cannot connote the lack
your wrinkled purse has won,
a grass-tainting inactive dew?

II

Lady, old fog is your friend.
Though he strokes your road's
bald lamp, seeking such heat
as between electrodes
a bright thread may distend.

Lady, old fog is your friend.
Though he breathes like a field
too anxious for his wheat
he'll have your wound healed.
You ask does his mist mend.

Lady, old fog is your friend.
Though you collapse inside
with odour of hide and meat
you see subtly magnified
seamy cells blurringly blend.